JEB STUART SPEAKS:

AN INTERVIEW WITH
LEE'S CAVALRYMAN

MAJOR JAMES EWELL BROWN STUART

Valentine Museum
Richmond, Virginia

JEB STUART SPEAKS:

AN INTERVIEW WITH
LEE'S CAVALRYMAN

BY

BERNICE-MARIE YATES

 White Mane Publishing Company, Inc.

This White Mane Publishing Company, Inc. publication
was printed by
Beidel Printing House, Inc.
63 West Burd Street
Shippensburg, PA 17257 USA

In respect for the scholarship contained herein, the acid-free paper used in this book meets the guidelines for permanence and durability of the Committee on Production Guidelines for Book Longevity of the Council on Library Resources.

For a complete list of available publications
please write
White Mane Publishing Company, Inc.
P.O. Box 152
Shippensburg, PA 17257 USA

Library of Congress Cataloging-in-Publication Data

Yates, Bernice-Marie, 1947–
    Jeb Stuart speaks : an interview with Lee's cavalryman / by
Bernice-Marie Yates.
        p.   cm.
    Includes bibliographical references (p.   ) and index.
    ISBN 1-57249-041-1   (alk. paper)
    1. Stuart, Jeb, 1833–1864.   2. Generals--Confederate States of
America--Biography.   3. Confederate States of America. Army-
-Biography.   4. United States--History--Civil War, 1861–1865-
-Cavalry operations.   5. Imaginary interviews--United States.
I. Title.
E467.1.S9.Y38   1997
973.7'3'092--dc21
[B]   96-39492
                                                                 CIP

PRINTED IN THE UNITED STATES OF AMERICA

For my students—past, present and future.

Table of Contents

List of Illustrations

Preface

This book is a self-interview with Major General James Ewell Brown Stuart, C.S.A. *Jeb Stuart Speaks* presents for the first time this approach to the historical investigation of Stuart's entire life and career. The author asks the questions we all want to ask the most famous cavalryman from the Army of Northern Virginia. Using Stuart's own words, she brings Major General Stuart to life and subjects him to modern scholarly inquiry.

The self-interview or Gestalt psychological technique is defined by the psychologist, Richard W. Bailey, as a procedure which is

"... an adaptation of the "Empty Chair" technique which was originally popularized by Frederick Perls, M.D., in his book *Gestalt Therapy*, 1951. The objective of the technique was to help an individual get in touch with and "own" parts of the self that have not previously been integrated into the whole self. In this way the historian is attempting to record historical information in an interview format in order to achieve a more completely integrated understanding of a historical figure. The historian enters into a dialogue with the historical figure in an effort to give the reader a more integrated view of the historical figure. In the end, it is hoped, the reader will have a better sense of the "whole" person."

Obviously, the interview never actually occurred, but it could have taken place.

General Stuart's responses to the questions are taken from his letters and dispatches and from conversations penned by men who were under his command during the war years and knew him personally: Heros Von Borcke and John Esten Cooke. The author has utilized portions of the biography, *Jeb Stuart*, by John W. Thomason and excerpts from Henry Kyd Douglas' biography of Thomas Jonathan Jackson, *I Rode with Stonewall*, for clarity. The result of this Gestalt methodology is a blend of emotional depth and quiet strength in complete harmony to create a powerful interpretation of this exciting historical figure.

Acknowledgments

It is with heartfelt thanks that I would like to express my gratitude to the following people and institutions for their encouragement, support and generosity of time:

Col. James Ewell Brown Stuart IV, Mrs. Adele Mitchell, Dr. Richard W. Bailey, Ms. Janet Davis, Mrs. Erlene Albanese, Mr. David McCormick, Mrs. Rebecca Rose, Mr. Guy R. Swanson, Mrs. Corrine Hudgins, Ms. Petie Bogen-Garrett, Ms. Theresa Roane, Mr. C. Vaughan Stanley, Ms. Julie Cline, Mr. Lee Shepard, Ms. Ann Marie Price, Mrs. Daryl Ann Humrichouser, Ms. Susan Walker, and Mr. Michael J. Winey.

Drew University Library
Madison, New Jersey

Fairfax Museum and Visitors Center
Fairfax, Virginia

Fairleigh Dickinson University Libraries
Madison and Teaneck, New Jersey

Library of Congress
Washington, D.C.

National Archives
Washington, D.C.

The Museum of the Confederacy
Richmond, Virginia

The United States Military Academy Archives
West Point, New York

The United States Army Military History Institute
Carlisle Barracks, Pennsylvania

Virginia Historical Society
Richmond, Virginia

The State Library of Virginia
Richmond, Virginia

Valentine Museum
Richmond, Virginia

Washington and Lee University
Lexington, Virginia

Warren County Public Library
Belvidere, New Jersey

Dr. Martin K. Gordon, my editor

and last but certainly not least, my mother, Mrs. John Yates.

Introduction

What attributes distinguished James Ewell Brown Stuart from other generals of his era?

The answer can be found by examining his military career, reviewing his intense undying loyalty to a cause, or even his fanatical attitude toward the concept of nineteenth century American chivalry but most interesting were his unpretentious humanistic qualities which placed him beyond other men.

James Ewell Brown Stuart was an enigma, a man of complex contradictions.

Honor, duty and country meant everything to him, yet he surrendered his oath as an officer of the United States of America for the new Confederate States of America.

He was a formidable foe in battle whether in defense of his honor, the defense of a lady, or the defense of his Virginia. Yet, he was sensitive to beauty.

He loved music and would sing to his men as they awaited battle. He loved art and sought the aesthetic in everything from Dundee, the estate of the Price family, to the lace on a token handkerchief from an admirer. He loved literature, especially poetry and would write creative verse from the whimsical to the profound. He loved to gather flowers from the rustic countryside; this beautiful pastime became his symbol of chivalry.

He was a staunch family man, but his duty called him away. Even when his little daughter died due to an illness during the war, he felt his higher duty was to all the mothers and children of the South. This is not to imply that he did not grieve for the loss of his own child. He did grieve deeply and when his ebb of emotional strength waivered he stated his desire to join his little Flora.

This was a man who championed and loved life, but making war was his lifework.

This was a man who had a reputation as a ladies' man, but in reality loved one women and remained faithful to her, Flora Cooke Stuart, his wife.

Here was a gentleman whose appearance expressed a flamboyant and extroverted personality yet, in fact, he was a private person who would regularly go off alone.

Here was a general whose actions in war and love of frivolity would suggest an immoral nature, but in fact he was deeply and penitently religious.

Stuart was the cavalryman's cavalryman. He never asked any subordinate officer or member of the rank and file to do anything he would not do himself. This attitude would ultimately lead to his death at the age of thirty-one. He became a role model for his men, not an icon like Lee or Jackson. He was a knight-errant and a gentleman eminently worthy of your acquaintance.

Stuart Chronology

1833

February 6
—James Ewell Brown Stuart is born at "Laurel Hill" in Patrick County, Virginia

1848-1850

Attends Emory and Henry College

1850-1854

July 1850
—Enters the United States Military Academy, West Point, New York

June 1854
—Graduates 13th in a class of 46

1854-1861

1854-1861
—United States Cavalry stationed on the frontier: Texas to Kansas

November 14, 1855
—Marries Flora Cooke, daughter of Colonel [Major General, U.S.A.] Philip St. George Cooke

September 1857
—Birth of daughter, Flora

1859
—Sells cavalry saber device to the United States government
—Participates in the capture of John Brown at Harpers Ferry, [West] Virginia
—Returns to Kansas

June 26, 1860
—Birth of son, James Ewell Brown Stuart, Jr., "Jimmy" [formerly named Philip St. George Cooke Stuart]

May 3,1861
—Resigns commission in the United States Cavalry at the rank of captain

May 8, 1861
—Becomes commissioned lieutenant colonel of the infantry in the Provisional Army of Virginia

May 24, 1861
—Becomes colonel in the Confederate cavalry, establishing the First Virginia Cavalry

September 24, 1861
—Promoted to brigadier general of the cavalry after First Manassas
—By the end of 1861, the cavalry is a highly efficient and superbly trained fighting unit.

1862

June 12–16
—Peninsula Campaign: Stuart's ride around McClellan

June 25–July 1
—Seven Days Campaign: Malvern Hill

July 25
—Promoted to major general

August–September
—Prior to Second Manassas, Stuart obtains full command of the cavalry of Northern Virginia
—Brilliant performances at Second Manassas, Catlett's Station, Groveton and Sharpsburg [Antietam]

October 10–11
—Chambersburg Raid

November 3
—Death of daughter, Flora

November 19–December 13
—Fredericksburg Campaign

1863

May 1–4
—Battle of Chancellorsville
—Temporary command of Jackson's Corps

June 5
—"The Grand Review"

June 9
—Battle of Brandy Station

July 1–3
—Battle of Gettysburg

October 9
—Birth of second daughter, Virginia Pelham

August–December
—Continued reconnaissance activities

1864

Spring
—Stuart at his best, bringing General R. E. Lee important information on Lieutenant General U. S. Grant's movements

May 5–7
—The Battle of the Wilderness

May 9
—Sheridan begins moving from Spotsylvania toward Richmond; Stuart mounts his final battle.

May 11
—Stuart and Sheridan clash at Yellow Tavern.
—Stuart is mortally wounded by John Huff, a dismounted Federal cavalryman.

May 12
—Stuart dies in Richmond at the Brewer House.

May 13
—Stuart's funeral and burial at Hollywood Cemetery

Session I

The Creation of a Cavalryman

Setting of the Interview:
Winter 1995
The United States Military Academy
at
West Point, New York

Interviewer: Good afternoon, General Stuart. Thank you for coming to the twentieth century for this interview.

GEN. STUART: Thank you for the invitation to be interviewed. It has been more than one hundred and thirty years since I have spoken candidly.

Interviewer: I would like to start now with your permission, General Stuart.

GEN. STUART: Please do, I have much I would like to relate.

Interviewer: General Stuart, your last day on this earth was May 12, 1864. Did you feel that you had fulfilled your earthly mission?

GEN. STUART: When I was laying on my death bed I told President Jefferson Davis that I was willing to go if I had fulfilled my duty to God and country. I tried to live my life by the motto of my alma mater, here, at the United States Military Academy, "Duty, Honor and Country." But, it is for you, the historian, to say if I completed my destiny.[1]

Interviewer: Yes, sir, it seems you did complete your role provided by divine providence. Yet, General did you have any regrets?

GEN. STUART: Yes, I regretted that I could not have seen my loving wife and children before my demise. I was concerned for them. I asked my good friend, Von Borcke, to look after my family after I was gone and be the same true friend to my wife and children that he had been to me. My dear Von, I loved no man better. God's will be done.[2]

Interviewer: Your untimely death was a severe blow to your wife. However, Mrs. Stuart was a strong woman, who went on to maintain your lasting memory in the public eye.

GEN. STUART: I love her very much!

MAJOR JOHANN AUGUST HEINRICH HEROS VON BORCKE

Eleanor S. Brockenbrough Library
The Museum of the Confederacy
Richmond, Virginia

Interviewer: General Stuart, tell me about your mother and father and your childhood.

GEN. STUART: I was born at "Laurel Hill" my family's plantation in Patrick County, Virginia, on February 6, 1833. I was the eighth child of eleven children and the youngest boy. My father, Archibald Stuart, was a veteran of the War of 1812 and a lawyer. He was an assemblyman to the Virginia legislature, the Virginia Conventions of 1829-30 and 1850 as well as a representative to the United States Congress from Patrick County. My mother was Elizabeth Letcher Pannill Stuart from Chalk Level, Pittsylvania County, Virginia.

My mother's family was well established in the Virginian squirearchy. You will recall our family ties to Governor John Letcher, 1860-1864.[3]

Interviewer: What qualities do you feel you inherited from your mother and father?

GEN. STUART: I think I inherited from my mother the love of beauty in nature. Did you know that I kept a scrapbook of flowering plants from 1855-1857, while I was stationed on the frontier?[4]

Interviewer: Yes, I did. I had the opportunity to see it on a recent trip to Richmond. I was truly impressed, but I didn't mean to interrupt you General, please go on.

GEN. STUART: I believe that most importantly my mother influenced my deep religious convictions. My belief in God sustained me through many difficult situations. My mother often said that I possessed my father's wit, charm and singing voice. In short, a joie de vivre! But more substantially there was an obligation to maintain a natural progression of leadership inherent in Southern men of stature. This was a principle established through a strong character and a determination to succeed—to take chances and not accept defeat. Leadership without character is worthless.[5]

Interviewer: I agree General. Would you tell me something about your early education?

GEN. STUART: Yes, I studied with Mr. Buchanan and then at a boarding school named "Hillcrest" with Dr. George Whitfield Painter from 1846–1847. At the age of fifteen, I volunteered for the Mexican War, but was not accepted on account of my youth. Therefore, I started my tenure at Emory and Henry College from 1848–1850. In 1850 I entered West Point.[6]

Interviewer: How did you feel about your tenure here at West Point?

GEN. STUART: The natural beauty of the situation of West Point, the picturesque mountains' scenery, the magnificent view of the Hudson, the delightful river breezes, all conspired to render our life agreeable, to say nothing of other advantages afforded for intellectual culture and polish.

> To tinge with rainbow hues our future skies,
> And bid each thought suggest a paradise;
> To give to every hope a fairer tint,
> And melt with rapture e'en a heart of flint.[7]

I think the climate suited me better than that of Virginia. One would think that place situated as this was, in the heart of free-soil Yankeedom, was strongly tainted with that spirit, but quite to the contrary was the fact there was a strong Southern feeling prevalent on the Point no doubt far more than Mr. Van Buren ever cherished. In a word with us all was harmony . . . in the language of one worthy of being quoted, "know no East, no West no North, no South." West Point would be perfect, if located in Virginia.[8]

Interviewer: Did West Point provide you with the type of education that reinforced your squirearchy roots and establishing your knight-errant reputation during your years of service to the Confederacy?

GEN. STUART: I believe fours years training at West Point would be the making of a chivalric man. It would be the means of strengthening his constitution, establishing his health, and making him, both physically and mentally, emphatically making him a man. For one to succeed here, all that is required is an ordinary mind and application; the latter is by far the most important and desirable of the two. For men of rather obtruse intellect, by indomitable perseverance, have been known to graduate with honor; while some of the greatest geniuses of the country have been found deficient, for want of application, Edgar A. Poe for instance. We had a few of the chivalrous as well as some rank abolitionists but they took good care to be quiet.[9]

> To horse, to horse! the sabers gleam,
> High sounds our bugle call,
> Combined by honor's sacred tie,
> Our watchword, "laws and liberty!"
> Forward to do or die.[10]

I admire Sir Walter Scott.

Interviewer: Did you have your share of demerits at West Point?

GEN. STUART: Yes, I would uphold my honor, if questioned. I would call out the fellow and challenge him to physical retribution.

Interviewer: I suppose a case could be presented for pugilism as a form of exercising one's tactical or even intellectual abilities.

GEN. STUART: On one occasion I recall being taken to account by William P. Sanders, class of 1856. So great was our disparity in size that my friend Rogers wanted me to insist upon taking a club, which I persisted in refusing. I told him it was a matter of little consequence whether I whipped or was whipped, and I would not have the appearance of seeking an advantage for the sake of a victory . . . we were both pretty badly bruised—my eye had completely closed up and my arms were as weak as water. Finding myself completely "hors de combat," as "discretion is the better part of valor," I acknowledged myself whipped. This ended the fight. We had no fears of being caught as it was too early for officers to frequent such a secluded spot. The whole episode was a matter of honor for both Sanders and myself.[11]

Interviewer: When did you graduate from West Point?

GEN. STUART: In 1854 I graduated and in the fall of the same year I was attached as brevet 2nd lieutenant to the Regiment Mounted Riflemen. I was ordered to join my company in western Texas.[12]

JAMES EWELL BROWN STUART, 1854

SESSION II

The Prewar Years

Setting of the Interview:
Winter 1995
Harpers Ferry
National Historical Park
at
Harpers Ferry, West Virginia

JAMES EWELL BROWN STUART
(Civilian Suit)

Eleanor S. Brockenbrough Library
The Museum of the Confederacy
Richmond, Virginia

GEN. STUART: Good morning, I'm glad you did not have difficulty locating the arsenal. I have not thought
about this place in a very long time.

Interviewer: Good morning to you, General Stuart. I have been
here many times before but I never had the experiences you had as an officer in both the United
States Army and the Army of Northern Virginia. I
would like to talk to you about these adventures
later, but now I would like you elaborate about
your frontier experiences?

GEN. STUART: Yes. Before I reached my company on October
31st [1854] I was promoted to a 2nd lieuten-
ancy in Company G. I joined the same regiment
February 3 of 1855, on an expedition against
the Muscalero Apaches, commanded by Major
Simonson, F.M.R. about 100 miles north of Fort
Davis. I rode on horseback from Corpus Christi,
Texas to that point between the December 28,
1954 and February 3, 1955. I remained on that
cold winter's campaign in the field and almost
constantly in the saddle until May 8 of that year
when I received my transfer as 2nd lieutenant to
one of the new regiments, First Cavalry, for which
I started immediately traversing on horseback
the distance from Fort Davis to Indianola, Texas.
I joined my Company H at Jefferson Barracks, Missouri, in June and was immediately assigned to
the command of it and to the duty of acting adjutant. A few days after I was also assigned to
the command of Company C, I continued per-
forming this three fold duty, till June 17 when
the regiment was ordered to Fort Leavenworth,
to which point I conducted the two companies I

commanded by steamer, arriving there June 23, 1955. On July 5 I was appointed regular quartermaster in addition to the command of two companies. On August 7 and September 10 I was relieved by the proper officers of the companies of cavalry under Colonel Sumner on Sioux Expedition on September 19 as chief quartermaster of the command, returning to Leavenworth with that command November 4, 1855.[1]

Interviewer: Sir, wasn't it about this time that you and Mrs. Stuart were married?

GEN. STUART: I married Miss Flora Cooke, daughter of Colonel Philip St. George Cooke, commanding officer of the Second Dragoons with headquarters at Fort Riley, Kansas Territory, on November 14, 1855. The next day we left for Fort Leavenworth, Kansas Territory. It was a whirlwind courtship, we married after being introduced in the summer. I was twenty-two and Mrs. Stuart was nineteen.[2]

Interviewer: Please continue with your frontier experiences.

GEN. STUART: By December 20, 1855, I was promoted to first lieutenant. In 1856, I was mostly in the field in Kansas during her difficulties acting as quartermaster and commissary.[3]

Interviewer: General, was this when you first became acquainted with John Brown?

GEN. STUART: Yes, Brown and his band were active in May of 1856 in the Pottawatomie Creek area. In the spring of 1857, I began the Cheyenne Expedition on May 20 and ended on September 10. During that expedition I, in common with the rest, endured the greatest hardship and deprivation of food and water. At the Battle of Solomon's Fork, which occurred in this campaign July 29, 1857, after pursuing the enemy seven miles, I received a severe wound in the centre of my breast from a pistol in the hands of an Indian whilst rushing between him and a brother officer in imminent peril which left me disabled for several weeks. Colonel Sumner, to my surprise, made no mention of that

GENERAL PHILIP ST. GEORGE COOKE

National Archives

incident in his report, but he informed me several months after that he did not hear of it. It was so generally known and applauded at the time, that I presume everyone took it for granted he knew it. At any rate the incident can be proved by Lieutenant McIntyre and Lieutenant Lomax of my regiment who saw it, and the former afterward; gave the death blow to the Indian though badly wounded by me. The officer rescued had dismounted to fire at this Indian, then standing, with greater accuracy—but his pistol hung fire and in this predicament the Indian rushed at him, and I dashed between with my sabre giving him a severe head cut—but his pistol was discharged not two feet from my body, covering my face and person with powder. The ball has never been extracted.[4]

Interviewer: That was certainly a dangerous mission. But, sir, what other important events occurred in your life during 1857 and 1858?

GEN. STUART: In September of 1857, our daughter Flora was born. I always called her La Petite or La Pet. I was a doting father at the age of twenty-four. Although in command of a company, I was again, much against my will, made commissary at Fort Leavenworth for General Harney's brigade, it being alleged by his assistant adjutant general that I was best fitted for the place—I remained in that capacity till my company having in the meantime been ordered to Fort Riley, I followed it resuming command December 16 and on the next day was detailed with twenty men to escort the Santa Fe mail to the crossing of Arkansas. I returned from this severe service January 4, 1858, and resumed command of my company which I held until March 31 when the captain relieved me. My company belonged to the "Utah Forces" and I accompanied it under Major Sedgwick doing the duties of quartermaster commissary and doctor of his command. It marched in advance of all the reinforcements, leaving Fort Riley on

GENERAL ROBERT EDWARD LEE

Portrait by Theodore Pine
Washington and Lee University

May 29, 1858, arriving there August 29 just three
months from time of departure. On the third day
of the following January we received orders suddenly for two companies, my company was one,
to repair immediately to the vicinity of the town
of Fort Scott, Kansas Territory, to aid the civil au-
thorities in arresting crime and bringing offend-
ers to justice. We made a forced march in very
severe weather of 125 miles when we received a
telegraphic countermand from the president
[Buchanan] to return to our post. We arrived at
Fort Riley on January 16, 1859.[5]

Interviewer: How would you describe your frontier movements
in 1859?

GEN. STUART: Actually uneventful. It was not until October when
I happened to be in Washington that the year be-
came momentous.

Interviewer: Why were you in Washington?

GEN. STUART: I had the honor to propose to assign all my right,
title and interest in my invention secured by
patent—entitled "improved method of attaching
sabres to belts" to the War Department of the
United States of America. I was paid the sum of
five thousand dollars.[6] While in Washington, I
heard of the Harper's Ferry affair accidentally.
Although scarcely anything was known except that
the Harper's Ferry Armory was in the possession
of a mob of, rumor said, over 3,000 men, still it
was pretty generally surmised that is was a servile insurrection.

As soon as I heard of it, I volunteered my services
to the Secretary of War and General [Robert E.] Lee,
who at that time was a colonel in the United States
Army, to accompany him to render any service I
could. He accepted my services and we left almost
immediately after for the scene of difficulty. I had
barely time to borrow a uniform coat and sabre—
and no time to drop a line to Flora at Richmond.
General Lee was off in quite as much haste. I stayed
at his house the day before at "Arlington." By mis-
take the regular troops, U.S. Marines, were ahead

of us twenty minutes. Another locomotive and car, however, sped us very rapidly in pursuit. We overtook them just below Harper's Ferry at twelve o'clock at night and dark. The insurgents had retired to and barricaded themselves in the fire engine house with several of the citizens of Virginia prisoners. I recall that it was raining slightly. In less than an hour General Lee had reconnoitred the place, relieved the militia guard stationed around the armory by a guard of marines, and determined upon his plan of operations which were successfully carried out early in the morning. I was constantly at General Lee's side and he told me all of his plans at the time and his reasons for them, and I gratefully acknowledged that he gave me all the prominence that was compatible with my position. General Lee was sent to command the forces at Harper's Ferry. I volunteered as his aide. I had no command whatever. The U.S. Marines were a branch of the naval force. There was not an enlisted man of the army on hand. Lieutenant Green was sent in command of the marines. Major Russell had been requested by the secretary of navy to accompany the marines, but being a paymaster could exercise no command—yet it was his corps. If General Lee had put me in command of the storming party, it would have been an outrage to Lieutenant Green which would have rung through the navy for twenty years. Lieutenant Green was the commander of the marines—and of course, was entitled to command the storming party—as well might they send him out to command my company of cavalry. At any rate, I was deputed by General Lee, on the morning of the eighteenth to read to the leader, then called Smith, a demand to surrender immediately and I was instructed after his refusal, which he expected, to leave the door and wave my cap at which signal he had directed the storming party to rush up and batter open the doors and capture the insurgents at the point of the bayonet. He cautioned the stormers particularly to discriminate between the insurgents and their prisoners.[7]

Interviewer: Sir, were you able to carry out your orders?

GEN. STUART: Yes, a brief cease-fire prevailed at the time. I approached the door, in the presence of 2,000 spectators, and told Mr. Smith, I had a communication for him from General Lee. He opened the door about four inches and placed his body against the crack with a cocked carbine in his hand. Incidentially, after his capture he remarked that he could have wiped me out like a mosquito. Nevertheless, the parley was a long one. He presented his propositions in every possible shape with admirable tact, but all, amounting to the only condition he would surrender upon to be allowed to escape with his party. Many of the prisoners begged me with tears to ask General Lee to come and see him. I told them he never would, I knew, accede to any terms but those he had offered, and as soon as I could tear myself away from the importunities of the prisoners I left and waved my cap and the plan was carried out.

Interviewer: Did anyone recognize that John Smith was actually John Brown?

GEN. STUART: Well, in all due modesty, I omitted to mention what I really think was the greatest service I rendered the state.

Interviewer: What service are you referring to?

GEN. STUART: When Smith first came to the door I immediately recognized him as "Old Ossawattomie" Brown who had given us so much trouble out in Kansas. But it was not until he was knocked down and dragged out pretending to be dead, that I proclaimed it— in order that the vast multitude and the world would find out that John Smith was Old Brown. No one else could have identified him there but myself. I got his bowie knife from his person while he was "possuming," and kept it until my own demise.

Interviewer: After Brown and his band were captured, what did you do the rest of the day?

GEN. STUART: The same day about 11 or 12, General Lee requested me, as Lieutenant Green had charge of the prisoners as was officer of the guard, to take a few marines and go over to Old Brown's house four and one half miles off over in Maryland and see what there was there. He wished me to ride but as the marines walked I did so and discovered the magazine of pikes, blankets, clothing of every kind and utensils of every sort. I could only carry off the pikes, having but one wagon, of which there were from 1,000 to 1,500. When I got back I found Governor Wise had arrived. He came at one o'clock that day—extremely chagrined that all was over before his arrival.

Interviewer: What type of person was Governor Wise?

GEN. STUART: He was a queer genius. I called on him in Richmond once myself and once with my cousin, Peter Wilson Hairston. He had known my father. He gave a speech in Richmond after he returned from Harper's Ferry stating that General Lee was "fit for any command on earth." But in his message to the legislature, Governor Wise said and I quote: "At the Relay Place, I telegraphed to Colonel Lee to grant no terms—Colonel Lee granted no terms." end of quote. What gross and outrageous injustice to General Lee who, if he ever received such a dispatch, received it after the whole affair was over. You see the Old Fox makes out by implication that General Lee was acting in obedience to his orders in what General Lee did. This finished Wise with me!

Interviewer: What did you do during the subsequent days following this Harper's Ferry incident?

GEN. STUART: The next day I was occupied delivering the various orders of General Lee and other duties devolving on an "aide-de-camp." We marched the night after, General Lee, myself and Green with thirty marines, six miles and back on a false alarm among the inhabitants of a district called Pleasant

Valley. The prisoners having been turned over to the U.S. marshal, General Lee and the marines were ordered back to Washington. I went with him and that terminated my connection with Harper's Ferry until May of 1861.[8]

Interviewer: General, you did not mention why you volunteered to go to Harper's Ferry?

GEN. STUART: The feeling that acuated me was this: I felt duty bound to let no opportunity slip to do my native state service—particularly when menaced with a servile war. I felt that I did all that my position allowed me to do and for it I claim NOTHING, but if a bill had been passed in the legislature of Virginia, rewarding Green and not including me, I would have felt exceedingly mortified.

Interviewer: Were you present for John Brown's trial and later at his execution?

GEN. STUART: No, I had returned to the Kansas Territory with my family by the time he was brought to trial and execution. Nevertheless, I took great abuse in the Northern newspapers for having sabred Brown, which was a lie. Green complained to me afterwards that his sword was so dull, being a common dress sword, he could not hurt Brown with it. And my sabre, being a sample one in the ordnance office, was like a razor. So, if I had commanded the stormers (instead of Lieutenant Green) my sabre would have saved Virginia the expense of Brown's trial. General Lee, in his report, expressed his thanks to Russell, Green and myself. He mentioned my name first which in view of my being junior in rank was a significant compliment to me. General Lee deserved a gold medal from Virginia. I presumed no one but myself will ever know the immense but quiet service he rendered the state and the country before and after the particular attack for which all give praise.[9]

Interviewer: It is a well-known fact that John Brown had a radical reputation as an abolitionist, but you, sir, as a Southern gentleman reared in the "peculiar institution of slavery," did you ever own any slaves?

GEN. STUART: This is a question often asked of many of us who had the honor to serve the great state of Virginia. In late October 1855 while I stationed along the Big Blue River, I received notice that my father had died.[10] If you know anything of my family, you know of the many losses my father sustained and that the fortune of my family was greatly reduced. In January of 1856, I obtained a leave of absence from my post and returned to Virginia for the division of the estate. Mother received one third and the balance of the estate was divided between eight heirs. When we returned to Kansas, we took with us one woman, young, healthy and highly valued. After that I acquired a man from Dr. Bayless of Missouri, formally of Kentucky. During the spring of 1858, I found it necesary to dispose of the woman because of cruelity to our baby daughter. Then in November of 1859, the man asked to be sold among his own people in Kentucky and I agreed. So, you see the extent of our holdings of such property was dispersed of shortly after the Harper's Ferry incident.[11]

Interviewer: What about "Mulatto Bob"?

GEN. STUART: Mullato Bob was the property of my mother. He was my personal servant during the war years.

Interviewer: But, General, how did you feel about the institution of slavery?

GEN. STUART: I think I can say most truly that my wife and I regarded slavery as an ordinance not forbidden but recognized as God given. Nevertheless, we were not sorry when the two we owned found good homes elsewhere.[12]

Interviewer: Upon returning to the West, were you involved in other maneuvers against hostile Indians?

GEN. STUART: Yes, there was this incident on the Arkansas River in the summer of 1860 involving the Kiowa war-chief Litarki's tribe.[13]

Interviewer: What happened, sir?

GEN. STUART: We received a report that the Kiowa chief and his family, in all two lodges, were fleeing in the direction of Bent's Fort. I soon found the trail and commenced a rapid pursuit. In a short time I came in sight of them several miles ahead, just as they, having abandoned their lodge poles and other weighty articles of baggage, were prepared for more rapid flight. I saw that my pursuit, to be successful, must be rapid, and followed at full gallop. I gained very perceptibly on them, and after two hours and a half from Bent's Fort, during which I had traversed twenty-six miles, I was just about overhauling the body of Indians, when I recognized Captain Steele's detachment, who were returning to Bent's Fort, from two days' scout. They recognized us on nearer approach, and coming up, the two columns saluted each other with a shout and joined in pursuit of the common foe. Litarki was not with his band at the time, but the two warriors killed were his brother and son, and the squaws were his. I reached camp without the loss of a man or horse.[14]

Interviewer: This encounter with the Kiowas, was it your last confrontation with them?

GEN. STUART: No, in the summer of 1860 we made distinct demonstrations against them, the Comanches and other hostile Indians.

Interviewer: Your frontier days were quite exciting and even eventful.

GEN. STUART: Yes, it was eventful; more than we suspected at the time. The foregoing is, I know, very egotistical and I may have dealt on unimportant heads but it is true and you may extract such as answers the purpose of my history.[15]

Interviewer: General Stuart, by the spring of 1861 the nation was in great turmoil. It must have been a difficult decision for you to chose a side.

GEN. STUART: For my part I had no hesitancy from the first that, right or wrong, alone or otherwise, I would go with Virginia. Of course, every true patriot deplores even the possibility of disunion, yet let its blessings not be purchased at too great a price. Put equality and independence in one scale and

Union in the other, and if the latter out weighs the former, I for one would, like Brennus, throw my sabre in the scale consecrated by the principles and blood of our forefathers—our constitutional rights without which the Union is a mere mockery.[16]

Interviewer: How did you feel at this time, so far away from Virginia?

GEN. STUART: Anxious to be nearer the scene of operations. I did not believe that there was harmony enough of feeling to bind up the wounds already inflicted. When Virginia took her step, though reluctant, it was sudden and irrevocable.[17]

Interviewer: When did you finally resign your commission in the United States Army?

GEN. STUART: On May 3, 1861 from Cairo, Illinois, I wrote the following to Colonel Lorenzo Thomas: "From a sense of duty to my native State Virginia, I hereby resign my position as as officer in the Army of the United States."[18]

Interviewer: It must have been a difficult decision for you to resign your commission, how did you feel?

GEN. STUART: I felt that my duty was to serve Virginia and my family.

JAMES EWELL BROWN STUART
(Lieutenant, United States of America)

Eleanor S. Brockenbrough Library
The Museum of the Confederacy
Richmond, Virginia

SESSION III

The War Years

Setting of the Interview:
Winter 1995
Brandy Station Battlefield
Near
Culpeper, Virginia

GENERAL J. E. B. STUART

Cornelius Hankins, Artist
Virginia Historical Society
Richmond, Virginia

Interviewer: This truly is a beautiful area, Brandy Station. The site remains very much the same as it did when you and the others fought the greatest cavalry battle on the continent here.

GEN. STUART: Yes, I am actually quite surprised that the area retains much on its natural beauty.

Interviewer: You held a "Grand Review" here in June 1863, didn't you?

GEN. STUART: Yes, General [Robert E.] Lee reviewed the division the day before the fight.[1]

Interviewer: I have read that the "review" was a spectacular sight. Well, shall we get started with the final phase of the interview.

GEN. STUART: Yes, I am very proud of my career in the Confederate army.

Interviewer: What was your first appointment in the Confederate forces?

GEN. STUART: I was appointed lieutenant colonel of infantry in the Provisional Army of Virginia. I received marching orders with my appointment for Harper's Ferry where I was to be second in command, Colonel Jackson of the institute being my senior.[2]

Interviewer: The Colonel Jackson you mentioned, was he Thomas "Stonewall" Jackson of the Virginia Military Institute?

GEN. STUART: Yes. We became good friends.

Interviewer: It has been said that when General Jackson lay on his death bed he said that you should succeed him and command his corps, how did you feel about such an assignment?

GEN. STUART: I would rather know that Jackson said that, then have the appointment.[3]

LIEUTENANT GENERAL THOMAS JONATHAN JACKSON

National Archives
(#2-4)

Interviewer: What was your assignment at Harper's Ferry in May 1861?

GEN. STUART: There were 3, or 4,000 men at Harper's Ferry—so as you see I commanded a brigade at once.[4] About a week after I arrived in Harper's Ferry I changed my headquarters to Bolivar, a suburb of Harper's Ferry, where I had the cavalry concentrated [3 companies.] The remaining five of my command were detached—two at Point of Rocks, twelve miles below; one at Berlin Bridge on the Virginia side, six miles below; one at Sheperdstown; and one in Martinsburg. Eleven hundred Alabamians arrived and some Virginia troops, the Grayson Dare Devils included. The last were quartered with Captain Pendleton's [clergyman of Protestant Episcopal Church] company from Lexington. A. P. Hill was there as a colonel of volunteers.[5]

Interviewer: What was your impression of the atmosphere and attitude of the men in your command?

GEN. STUART: The greatest enthusiasm prevailed, and the determination to do or die was impressed on every man's features.[6]

Interviewer: During the next several weeks, what activities occupied your time?

GEN. STUART: Bivouac was the order of the day. I had been so constantly in the saddle that for several days I had no time to write except officially. Our presence in Berkley County for two weeks had a wonderful effect with the good people of that region. By mid June, General J. E. Johnston notified me to retire from Camp Clover to Winchester. It was accomplished on short notice and the march was made in one night. I got there ahead of him and returned along his flank covering his march towards Winchester. We turned suddenly across from that route to meet General Robert Patterson's division crossing at Williamsport. After a long and fatiguing march my advance scouts met those of the enemy, the latter being in much larger force, eighty men to

ten, nevertheless retired first and spread con-
sternation and alarm in the enemy's camp by the
news of Virginia forces advancing. Old George H.
Thomas [Major General] was in command of the
cavalry of the enemy. I would have liked to have
hanged him as a traitor to his native state. The
day before General J. E. Johnston had me ten to
twelve miles in advance at Martinsburg. I sent to
him to say he could get to that place but for fear
of being surrounded he had taken a position to
meet the enemy near Winchester. I took a 100
men to reconnoitre the enemy and take view of
his numbers. I felt sure that somewhere there a
battle would be fought.[7]

Interviewer: Did you personally feel any apprehension at this
time?

GEN. STUART: Yes, I had the greatest anxiety manifested for the
arrival of my father-in-law, Phillip St. George
Cooke. He was regarded as the "ne plus ultre" of
a cavalry officer. I often questioned—Why doesn't
he come? If he could have only seen things in
their true and real light, which was difficult to do
so far off. He was wanted here very much. He was
highly complimented everywhere and would soon
take a foremost stand in the state defense. Why
didn't he come? He would have been on the same
side as his children. Principle, interest and affection demanded his immediate resignation and
return to his native state.[8]

Interviewer: But, General Cooke remained in the United States
Cavalry; it must have been a difficult decision for
him.

GEN. STUART: Perhaps. However, he would regret it but once,
and that would be continuously.[9]

Interviewer: General Stuart, why did you change your son's
name?

GEN. STUART: When our son was born in 1860, his name was
Phillip St. George Cooke Stuart but I could not
understand why our son's namesake remained
loyal to a country that denied and invaded his

native state Virginia. I thought it would be an ir-
reparable injury to the boy and embitter the last
days of his father who up to this moment had
labored to leave nought for him to be ashamed
of. I suggested several names to my wife and that
she should decide on the name. He was renamed
James Ewell Brown Stuart, Jr. We called him
"Jimmie."[10]

Interviewer: What legacy did you leave to your son?

GEN. STUART: I wanted my wife to tell my boy when I was gone
how I felt and wrote and tell him never to do anything which his father would be ashamed of—
never to forget the principles for which his father
struggled. We were sure to win, but what the sacrifices were to be we could not tell, but if the enemy held every town and hilltop Southern subju-
gation would be no nearer its consummation than
now.[11] I wrote to my wife: "When I am gone train
up my boy in the footsteps of his father and tell
him never to falter in implicit faith in Divine Providence. . . . It will be gratifying to me while living
to know that you have respected my wishes, and
it will console me in death to feel that the birth-
right and heritage I leave to you and mine will be
preserved as I desired."[12]

Interviewer: General, you must have harbored strong emotional feelings against your father-in-law to cause
you to change your son's name. Did you ever hope
you would meet on the battlefield?

GEN. STUART: Perhaps, I did desire a face-to-face battlefield
encounter.

Interviewer: General, many family members during the war
were on opposite sides. Take the Kentucky
Breckinridge brothers for example. The Confederate brother was captured and forced to surrender to his Unionist brother during the Battle of
Atlanta.[13] Consequently, if General Cooke and you
had met on the field, would it have been a battle
of knightly combat testing the tenents of might
verse right?

GEN. STUART: Divine providence never gave us the opportunity to decide the answer to that question. Yet, there were a few times we came close to an encounter. I suppose the nearest we came to confrontation was during the Peninsula Campaign.

Interviewer: It has been said that the anticipation of battle is often worst than the battle. Do you agree?

GEN. STUART: Prior to Harper's Ferry things were hastening to a crisis. Everyday, sometimes twice a day, I heard the enemy drawing a little closer. He [the Federals] had not reached the Potomac. General Johnston himself wrote to me every day, and I had little doubt that at the moment the enemy was near Johnston would march out near me and meet him [the Federals] instead of waiting to be attacked at Harper's Ferry. Everyone was delighted with our camp here. There was little time for sleep. But, when I did get to sleep, which was not often, I slept like a log. On one night when a patrol arrived from Sheperdstown and reported to me to know if I had any orders I said, in my sleep: "No, all I want is to have my horse shod." At another time a man named Dugan came about one at night to see me on what he called important business. I said to Peter W. Hairston, "Give him an audience and let him go." I could not have answered better if awake.[14]

Interviewer: I have read that the ladies of Maryland were especially kind to you because of your chivalrous attributes. Is this true?

GEN. STUART: If you could have seen the strawberries, bouquets, and other nice things the ladies sent me, you would think me pretty well off. The young men of the regiment wonder why it was that I would be the recipient of so much favor—they forgot that rank will tell. These ladies regarded us as knights, their champions. The cavalry had some spirited engagements with the enemy, with glorious results. The ladies of Maryland made a great fuss, begging autographs, etc.[15] We protected and honored these ladies and they showered us with attention and gratitude. I found the most demonstrative joy on the part of most of the ladies. Chivalry had its rewards.

Interviewer: General, when did you actually have an encounter with the Federals?

GEN. STUART: On June 20, [1861] I received intelligence of a regiment having crossed at Williamsport [Maryland.] I mounted my command and put after them. When I reached that point, however, there were none this side of the river. A large force was on the other side, and as General Johnston had instructed me to create the impression that he was going to attack the place, I flew around generally laying of batteries, giving directions for attack etc.; a shower of minie bullets was falling all around me. The enemy made its dispositions immediately for defense, and you would have been amused at the sham fight on my part. We fired not a gun but when I told two of my men where to place their pieces of artillery and how to range them, you ought to have seen how I made a battalion of infantry run. The enemy retired toward Hagerstown, Maryland. The only solution I knew was that they were going to concentrate at Washington.[16]

Interviewer: General, when did you make your first substantial capture?

GEN. STUART: I was occupying the advance post of Johnston's army only two miles from the enemy's lines. Johnston was three and a half miles behind me—in battle array. The enemy was striking tents preparatory to move. During those last two days my regiment had been in the midst of the enemy. On July 2, I captured one whole company, the Fifteenth Pennsylvania officers and all—two privates of Second Cavalry and a surgeon, including forty-eight stands of arms and ammunition.[17]

Interviewer: General Stuart, how did you learn of the General McDowell's replacement and other information pertaining to the Union movements?

GEN. STUART: When I reached Fairfax Court House on July 23, I sent scouting parties around. The enemy's retreat continued in utter disorder into Washington City; 50,000 were said to be engaged. I obtained information from Arnold Harris [Confederate spy.] He said McClellan had been ordered to succeed McDowell at once and that there was no force this side of Alexandria; 50,000 were to be mustered out of service in fifteen days. Also, Banks had been ordered to relieve Patterson.[18]

Interviewer: How did you feel about obtaining this information?

GEN. STUART:I was doing my duty, and upholding the honor of Virginia.

Interviewer: What were the operations of your regiment in the Battle of First Manassas?

GEN. STUART:I received my orders to charge the enemy's flank and proceed immediately across the run to his left flank, but finding that it would be easier to attain his right flank, I immediately returned and marched rapidly towards the heaviest fire. As I approached the ground General Jackson, whose brigade was then engaged, sent me word to protect his flanks, particularly his left flank. I divided the regiment, giving Major Swan half, I had about 300 men on duty, and with the remainder hurried up to Jackson's left, leaving his right to Swan. Entering a skirt of woods, I received intelligence that the enemy was rapidly outflanking us. I hastened forward through several fences just as a regiment dressed in red was running in disorder towards a skirt of woods where the fire had been heaviest. I took them to be ours, and exclaimed with all my might: "Don't run, boys; we are here." They paid very little attention to this appeal. When passing in column of twos through a narrow gap to gain the same field and very close to them, I saw in their hands the U.S. flag. I ordered the charge, which was handsomely done, stopping their flank movement and checking the advance upon Jackson. I rallied again for another charge, as only a portion of my command was in the first, owing to the difficulty of closing up; but finding the enemy had gained the woods to my right and front, leaving no ground for charging, I retired to the next field to give them another dash if they penetrated beyond the woods, which, however, they did not attempt. In this encounter the enemy's line, or rather column, was broken and many killed. Captain Carter's company, on which the heaviest of the action fell, lost nine men killed or mortally wounded, and wounded, and eighteen horses killed. Captain Carter's horse was shot dead as he was gallantly leading his company into the enemy. Of the gallantry of those engaged I cannot speak in too high terms. The regiment we charged was the Fire Zouaves, and I was informed by prisoners taken that their repulse by the cavalry began the panic so fearful afterwards in the enemy's ranks. Just after the cavalry charge our reinforcements arrived upon the field and formed rapidly on the right into line. The first was Colonel Falkner's regiment [Mississippians], whose gallantry came under my own observation. As these reinforcements formed I gradually moved off to the left, where I soon found myself joined by a battery, under the direction of Lieutenant Beckham, which my cavalry supported. This battery made great havoc in the enemy's ranks and finally put them in full retreat. The principal credit here was due to this battery; but having thrown forward vedettes far out on the eminences, the important information I was thus enabled to give the battery as to the position and movements must have contributed greatly to its success, and here I may add that this information was also sent back to the infantry, which was still far to our right, notifying them that the woods could be gained. The enemy was now in full retreat. I followed with the cavalry as rapidly as possible, but was so much encumbered with prisoners, whom I sent as fast as possible back to the infantry. My command was soon too much reduced to encounter any odds, but I nevertheless followed our success until I reached a point twelve miles from Manassas. By sending back so many detachments with prisoners, I now had but a squad left. The rear of the enemy was protected by a squadron of cavalry and some artillery. We cut off a great many squads, many of whom fired upon us as we approached, and the artillery gave us a volley of grape. One man of ours was killed and another wounded at this point. I had no idea how many prisoners were taken. I encamped that night on Sudley farm, where there was a large church, being used as a hospital by the enemy, containing about 300 wounded, the majority mortally. I cannot speak in too high praise of those whom I had the honor to command on the field, but to Mr. L. T. Brien and Mr. P. W. Hairston and J. F. Brown, having no commissions, whose meritorious conduct and worth I was especially indebted to for their valuable assistance. Of my regiment the acting chaplain, Reverend Mr. Ball, was conspicuously useful, while by attention was particularly attracted to the adjutant, Lieutenant W. W. Blackford; the Sergeant Major Philip H. Powers, and Lieutenant Cummings, whose good conduct on this as on every other occasion, obtained the highest commendation. Lieutenant Beckham, likewise, received high praise for the success of his battery, as he acted as gunner to each piece himself. In the pursuit, Lieutenant William Taylor alone captured six of the enemy with arms in their hands. A large number of arms, quantities of clothing and hospital stores, and means of transportation were found abandoned on the road; which of course, I commandeered.[19]

Interviewer: After the Confederate victory at Manassas, where did you place your headquarters?

GEN. STUART: For the next several weeks my headquarters was located at Munson's Hill. On August 28, as soon as it was fair light, I had a piece of rifled canon, Washington Battery [Artillery,] brought clandestinely in position to be on Bailey's Cross-Roads and fired four shots, distance being by the shots 1,350 yards. The shots took effect admirably, dispersing the entire force at that point, and developed what it was my object to ascertain—that they had no artillery there. Munson's Hill was a fine place for a battery and it was more capable of defense than Mason's Hill. The fire of artillery dispersed also a long line of skirmishers, who ran precipitately without being in the slightest danger from it shots. The First Regiment was at Falls Church, and I had directed its commander to hold himself in readiness to move up to my support, or act to the left, as circumstances indicated. Two companies of that regiment were ordered to occupy the ridge along Upton's. I sent back Beckhams's section of artillery, as the men were pretty well used up from fatigue and hunger. I decided at this point to send Major Johnson's two companies back to Mason's Hill to relieve the companies at that location. This was a fine line of defense; I mean the line passing through Munson's Hill and Mason's Hill. Every inch of the road was visible from here to Bailey's Cross-Roads.[20]

Interviewer: Did you have any large confrontations in this area?

GEN. STUART: Yes, against my West Point friend, Orlando M. Poe. On September 11, I started with the Thirteenth Virginia Volunteers, commanded by Major Terrill [305 men], one section of Rosser's battery, Washington artillery, and a detachment of the First Cavalry, under Captain Patrick, for Lewinsville, where I learned from my cavalry pickets that the enemy was posted with some force. My intention was to surprise them, and I succeeded entirely, approaching Lewinsville by the enemy's left and rear taking care to keep my small force an entire secret from their observation. I at the same time carefully provided against the disaster to myself which I was striving to inflict upon the enemy and felt sure that, if necessary, I could fall back successfully before any force the enemy might have, for the country was favorable for retreat and ambuscade. At a point nicely screened by the woods from Lewinsville, and a few hundred yards from the place, I sent forward under Major Terrill, a portion of his command stealthily to reach the woods at a turn of the road and reconnoiter beyond. This was admirably done, and the major soon reported to me that the enemy had a piece of artillery in position in the road just at Lewinsville commanding the road. I directed him immediately to post his rifleman so as to render it impossible for the cannoneers to and, the piece, and, if possible, capture it. During subsequent operations the cannoneers tried ineffectually to serve the piece, and finally, after one was shot through the head, the piece was taken off. While this was going on a few shots from Rosser's section at a cluster of the enemy a quarter of a mile off put the entire enemy was in full retreat, exposing their entire column to flank fire from our piece. Some wagons and a large body of cavalry first passed in hasty flight, the rifled piece and howitzer firing as they passed. Then came flying a battery, eight pieces of artillery [Griffin's], which soon took position about 600 yards to our front and right, and rained shot and shell upon us during the entire engagement, but with harmless effect, although striking very near. Then passed three regiments of infantry at double-quick, receiving in succession as they passed Rosser's unerring salutation, his shells bursting directly over their heads, and creating the greatest havoc and confusion in their ranks.

The last infantry regiment was followed by a column of cavalry, which at one time rode over the rear of the infantry in great confusion. The Union field general, and staff officers were seen exerting every effort to restore order in their broken ranks, and my cavalry vedettes, observing their flight, reported that they finally were rallied a mile and a half below, taking their position there, firing round after round of artillery from that position up the road where they supposed our columns would be pursuing them. Captain Rosser, having no enemy left to contend with, at his own request was permitted to view the ground of the enemy's flight, and found the road plowed up by his solid shot and strewn with fragments of shells; two men left dead in the road, one mortally wounded, and one not hurt taken prisoner. The prisoners said that havoc in their ranks was fearful, justifying what I saw myself of the confusion. Major Terrill's sharpshooters were by no means idle, firing wherever a straggling Yankee showed his head, and capturing a lieutenant [by Major Terrill himself], one sergeant, and one private, all of the prisoners were from the Nineteenth Indiana under Colonel Meredith, as I recall. The prisoners reported to me that General McClellan himself was present. Our officers and men behaved in a manner worthy of the highest commendation. Our loss was not a scratch to man or horse. I had no way of knowing the enemy's losses except it must have been heavy, from the effects of the shots. There were four dead or mortally wounded Federal soldiers found along with four others taken prisoners.[21]

Interviewer: General, did you have any communications with friends who remained in the Federal army at this time?

GEN. STUART: Yes, Poe left me an invitation to dine with him.

Interviewer: An invitation for dinner?

GEN. STUART: Yes, it said:

My Dear Beauty:

I have called to see you, and regret very much that you were not in. Can't you dine with me at Willard's tomorrow? Keep your "black horse" off me!

From your old friend,

Poe

Interviewer: Did you reply to his invitation?

GEN. STUART: Yes, of course.

MAJOR GENERAL FITZHUGH LEE
*Massachusetts Commandery Military
Order of the Loyal Legion and the
United States Army Military History Institute*

Interviewer: What did you say?

GEN. STUART: Dear Poe:

> I heard that you called, and hastened to see you, but as soon as you saw me coming you were guilty of the discourtesy of turning your back upon me. However, you probably hurried on to Washington to get the dinner ready. I hope to dine at Willard's, if not tomorrow, certainly before long.
>
> Yours to count on,
>
> Beauty.[22]

Interviewer: You never had the opportunity to dine with him at Willard's, did you?

GEN. STUART: No, unfortunately.

Interviewer: Why did he call you "Beauty"?

GEN. STUART: It was a nickname from West Point. In those days, I was something less than beautiful!

Interviewer: It was sad that the war created many enemies of friends.

GEN. STUART: Alas for human expectations![23]

Interviewer: What was the atmosphere like in your camp in the late autumn of 1861?

GEN. STUART: We were anxiously hoping for the enemy to advance and it was pretty certainly determined by them that they would advance before the end of the month of November. I thought it would be a combined land and naval attack on Evansport. We had two very successful cavalry scouts after the Yankees. One was Major William Martin who captured a captain, a lieutenant and thirty men and five loaded wagons and teams complete, containing corn, without a scratch to his own men. The second, Lieutenant Colonel Fitzhugh Lee, had a sharp fight with a party of fourteen. Brooklin, killing seven, mortally wounding one; capturing ten, three of whom were badly wounded. Lee's horse was shot dead under him. Fitz Lee's scout, Chichester, who accompanied him as a guide, was mortally wounded. Lee spoke in high terms of him. Poor Chichester's loss was a severe blow to us.[24]

Interviewer: General, would you tell me about the Dranesville incident of December 20, 1861?

GEN. STUART: We had a hard-fought battle. I had four pieces and four regiments, say 1,200 strong. The enemy had from five to ten regiments, six, or seven pieces artillery. They said 3,100. Finding heavy reinforcements arriving, I withdrew my command in perfect order from the field, carrying off nearly all the wounded. The enemy's loss was over fifty killed; our killed twenty-seven. They evacuated at dark. I returned to Centreville.[25]

Interviewer: General Stuart, is it true that you were introduced to Laura Radcliffe shortly after the Battle of Dranesville?

GEN. STUART: Yes, I became acquainted with Laura, her mother and two sisters while visiting my wounded men after the Battle of Dranesville. The women nursed the wounded men from the Dranesville encounter. Mrs. Radcliffe and her daughters lived about seven miles east of my winter quarters, I named "Camp Que Vive."

Interviewer: I have read that you cultivated a friendship with Laura and wrote to her frequently during the three-month period of your winter encampment. Is this true?

GEN. STUART: Mrs. Radcliffe and her daughters were kind and generous to my men as well as myself. Frequently the weather conditions prohibited actual visits and brief notes became a substitute. I recall that I received an invitation to dine with the ladies on Christmas Day 1861, but declined due to reconnoitering in the opposite direction. Often these ladies would invite us to dinner and I would extend the courtesy via a subordinate officer. Once I remember I sent Captain Thomas Rosser.[26]

Interviewer: Yes, General, I can understand the reason for your congenial hospitality in the gloom of the winter, but some historians have implied that there was a deep emotional attachment between you and Laura Radcliffe. Do you wish to address your critics?

GEN. STUART: My correspondence with the ladies was the type of correspondence which pertains to the position I held and which never could be obtained with me if I were a subordinate officer from such you would no doubt hear insinuation from. Such men have not sense enough to understand it but I am thankful to say I have. . . .[27] To be specific Miss Laura was employed in dangerous missions of reconnaissance for Colonel John S. Mosby and myself. It was true I was anxious to hear from her, by letter or in person, but frequently society and politics interfered with our communications.

Interviewer: What do you mean "society and politics interfered," sir?

GEN. STUART: I will be frank in my meaning in using the phrase "society and politics interfered." This style of literary flattery was commonplace and acceptible in the dictates of nineteenth century American society. Nevertheless, many people would misunderstand and chose to misconstrue the purest of intentions. Notwithstanding, the realities of war made social calls impracticable to say nothing of being dangerous. Therefore, society and politics interfered.

Interviewer: But, General Stuart you wrote poetry to Laura Radcliffe and carried a lock of her hair, were these actions conventional?

GEN. STUART: Yes, many women sent me tokens. Many other officers received tokens as well as I. These women revered us as their champion, their knights of the Confederacy.

Interviewer: How did Mrs. Stuart feel about these "tokens"?

GEN. STUART: Mrs. Stuart became victimized by insinuation. I told her the society of ladies will never injure your husband and that I ought to receive her encouragement.[28]

Interviewer: General, what type of anticipation did you feel as the summer of 1862 approached?

GEN. STUART: I thought that the next summer would probably be the most eventful in a century. We had to nerve our hearts for the trial with a firm reliance on God. We had to plant our feet firmly upon the platform of our unextinguishable hatred to the Northern Confederacy with determination to die rather than submit. What a mockery would such liberty be with submission. I, for one, though I stood alone in the Confederacy, without countenance or aid, would uphold the banner of Southern independence as long as I had a hand left to grasp the staff, and then die before submitting.[29]

Interviewer: Is it not true that through the winter of 1862 the armies did not see much action. The next large scale encounter was during the Peninsula Campaign. What role did the cavalry play in the Battle of Williamsburg?

GEN. STUART: In early May of 1862, the Battle of Williamsburg was fought and won on the fifth. A glorious affair, brilliantly achieved by the rear portion of our army [Longstreet.] On the fourth my brigade distinguished itself, and on the fifth its attitude and maneuvering under constant fire prevented the enemy's leaving the woods for the open ground, thus narrowing his [Federal] artillery scope of fire. I considered the most brilliant feat of the fifth to be a dash of the Stuart horse artillery to the front, and, coming suddenly under a galling fire of the enemy from the woods from a reinforcement of the enemy, wheeled into action sustaining in the most brilliant manner the fortunes of the day until the infantry could come to its support, and all the time under a countinuous infantry fire of 200 yards or less distance. I was not out of fire the whole day. The day before [May 4] the cavalry made several charges, and Lawrence Williams told the bearer of a flag of truce that I came within an ace of capturing my father-in-law. Our cavalry charged their cavalry handsomely and they were entirely routed, their artillery captured, the cavalry flag of the enemy captured, but the Fourth Virginia Cavalry lost its standard bearer and flag. Colonel Williams Carter Wickham was wounded on the fourth and Major William H. Payne was wounded on the fifth. The Floyd County Militia in Pelham's battery behaved in the handsomest style, astounding everyone beyond measure. The Third Cavalry [Colonel Thomas F. Goode] joined my brigade at this point. We were without rations, and therefore had to withdraw that night from the field, leaving our wounded with the ladies of Williamsburg. The enemy was driven from the field entirely.[30]

Interviewer: General, that was a marvelous victory; however your reputation for making the "Grand Rounds," the ride around of McClellan's army, was even more exciting. Where and when did these operations occur?

GEN. STUART: In preparation for the Battle of Mechanicsville, General Lee ordered me to reconnoiter the right flank and rear of McClellan's position astride the Chickamony. Leaving Hanover Court House on June 12, 1862 with 1,000 troopers including John S. Mosby, I went completely around the Federal army. We had ridden some one hundred miles around 100,000 men and lost only one man in our number, the gallant Captain William Latane.[31] I made the second "Grand Rounds" of McClellan's army recrossing the Potomac in the face of McClellan's forces in October of 1862. The Northern papers teem with the accounts of it, and lied a great deal, of course. I cannot give you an extended account of our many thrilling adventures in Pennsylvania—it was full of danger and yet consummated without a single man killed. It was a march without a parallel—ninety miles in thirty-six hours in one stretch besides the long march otherwise. We captured and paroled about 300 prisoners at Chambersburg, capturing several hundred horses, seized and brought over a number of public functionaires to be held as hostages for our own good citizens were being unlawfully detained by the Yankees.[32]

Interviewer: What was the reaction in Virginia to your daring tactics?

GEN. STUART: I was so pleased at Little Jimmie's HURRAH FOR STUART!

Yet, you ought to have heard Emmitsburg and Leesburg hurrahing for Stuart and showering bouquets and blessings. I never saw anything equal to it.[33]

Interviewer: What were your activites in early July 1862?

GEN. STUART: By July 5, I had been marching and fighting for one solid week, generally on my own hook, with the cavalry detached from the main body. I ran a gunboat from the White House and took possession. What do you think of that? We had been everywhere victorious and on July 3, I had the infinite gratification of slipping around to the enemy's rear and shelling his camp at Westover. If the army had been up with me, we would have finished his business. Late on the fourth, the enemy came under the protection of their gunboats. McClellan was badly whipped, but the fighting had not yet ended. General [George A.] McCall and General [John F.] Reynolds were taken.[34]

Interviewer: Would you please discuss the events surrounding the Verdiersville incident?

GEN. STUART: In retrospect, I can laugh about the incident now! Late in the evening on August 17, 1862, I was riding east on the Orange Plank Road with Major Fitzhugh, Major Von Borcke, Captain Mosby and Lieutenants Chiswell Dabney, and Gibson. We were on our way to join with Fitz Lee near Raccoon Ford. I really did not concern myself about John Pope's position west of Clark Mountain and the Rapidan River. We decided to stay the night in the tiny village of Verdiersville, although I was annoyed that we did not meet with Fitz Lee's brigade. I became concerned about Fitz Lee's absence and I sent Major Fitzhugh in search for him. At sunrise on August 18, a large body of cavalry from the very direction from which Lee was expected approached, crossing the Plank Road just below me and going directly toward Raccoon Ford. Of course I thought it was Lee as no Yankees had been about for a month, but, as a measure of prudence I sent down two men to ascertain.

Interviewer: Which two men did you send, sir?

GEN. STUART: I sent Mosby and Gibson. They had not gone 100 yards before they were fired on and pursued rapidly by a squadron. I was in the yard bareheaded, my hat being on the porch. I just had time to mount my horse and clear the back fence, having no time to get my hat or anything else. I lost my haversack, blanket, talma, cloak and hat, with the palmetto star. Too bad wasn't it? I escaped unscathed, but I was greeted on all sides with congratulations and "Where's your hat?" I intended to make the Yankees pay for that hat. Poor Fitzhugh was not so fortunate. He was captured four miles off under similar circumstances with his fine grey horse. He was exchanged in ten days, however. The escape of Von Borcke and Dabney from this scene was equally miraculous.[35]

Interviewer: General Stuart, did you make the Yankees pay for your hat?

GEN. STUART: Oh, yes!

Interviewer: What did you do, sir?

GEN. STUART: Well, I was still chagrined after a few days about the loss of my plumed hat and other personal effects to say nothing for the capture of my adjuant, Major Fitzhugh. I obtained permission to raid the railroad behind Pope's lines. On the morning of August 22, I crossed the Rappahannock at Waterloo Bridge and Hart's Ford with two guns and 1,500 men, from the brigades of Beverly Robertson and Fitzhugh Lee, less the Third and Seventh Virginia Cavalry. By dark, we had reached Auburn, near Catlett's Station. Darkness and a sudden storm seemed to hamper our operations, however I was able to obtain information as the location of Pope's baggage trains. The Ninth Cavalry attacked the camp and captured three hundred prisoners, money, a dispatch book, and other papers as well as General Pope's personal baggage, horses and other property.

Interviewer: What did you do with General Pope's personal property?

GEN. STUART: The next morning I showed off Pope's best coat and other things to General Jackson and his men. Then, to Jackson's amusement, I took a piece of paper and wrote Pope a communication.

Interviewer: Sir, do you remember what you said in the communication?

GEN. STUART: Yes, I think it went something like this: Major General John Pope Commanding, etc.

GENERAL: You have my hat and plume. I have your best coat. I have the honor to propose a cartel for a fair exchange of the prisoners.

Very respectfully,

(Signed) J. E. B. Stuart

Major General C.S.A.[36]

Interviewer: Were the "prisoners" exchanged?

GEN. STUART: Yes, without incident.

Interviewer: General, many times when large numbers of people come together even for the same purpose, there are personality conflicts. Did you find this true in your command?

GEN. STUART: Yes, if two men in my command had a disagreement, I would have them discuss the situation and compromise on a solution. However, no matter what you do, some people will remain disquieted.

Interviewer: Would you please discuss as to your most difficult subordinate officers?

GEN. STUART: Late in October of 1861, I found Beverly Robertson by far the most troublesome man I had to deal with.[37] However, by May of 1863, he proved himself an eminently fit brigadier general.[38] In the autumn of 1863, the difficulties with William E. Jones were finally resolved.

Interviewer: What difficulties did you have with William E. Jones?

GEN. STUART: Believing that Brigadier General W. E. Jones received his appointment without my recommendation, to take command at Winchester, I wanted him assigned to the command of the brigade, now commanded by Colonel Munford. I had the honor to state that in a paper concerning the organization of my division forwarded, I asked that Colonel Munford be appointed brigadier general to command that brigade. I had the honor to state further that I did not regard Brigadier General Jones as deserving this command or as a fit person to command a brigade of cavalry. I said this from a thorough acquaintance with Munford in command of that brigade I expected hearty cooperation, zealous devotion and indefatigable attention to his duty. With Brigadier General Jones I felt sure of opposition, insubordination, and inefficiency to an extent that would have in a short time ruined discipline and subverted authority in the brigade. I begged the Commanding General [R.E. Lee] to avert such a calamity in my division and if there were any who entertained different views in regard to General Jones, let such have the benefit of his services and his talents.[39] A trial having shown that Brigadier General W. E. Jones did not possess the qualities essential to a successful cavalry leader and commander, I begged leave to request that, as soon as the exigencies of the service will permit, one of the many colonels better deserving the position and better fitted to fill it be promoted to it and that he be transferred to other duty.[40]

Interviewer: Was Jones tranferred from your command?

GEN. STUART: On September 10, 1863, I was still requesting General Lee to consider the replacement of General Jones. In that letter I said: "I feel satisfied that I have not been mistaken in my estimate of an officer under my command in a single instance, and if you look over these letters you will agree with me." I regarded General Jones' assignment to that brigade over Munford as highly prejudicial to the service. I reminded General Lee how earnestly and persistently I entreated him and General Jackson to leave Munford in command. By October 1863, Jones was transferred to the Department of Western Virginia.[41]

MAJOR GENERAL BEVERLY HOLCOMBE ROBERTSON
*Massachusetts Commandery Military
Order of the Loyal Legion and the
United States Army Military History Institute*

MAJOR GENERAL WILLIAM EDMONDSON JONES
Library of Congress

MAJOR GENERAL THOMAS LAFAYETTE ROSSER
Massachusetts Commandery Military
Order of the Loyal Legion and the
United States Army Military Institute

Interviewer: By contrast there were many men whom you thought deserved promotions. General, would you comment on a few of these men?

GEN. STUART: As I previously stated, Thomas Munford certainly was very deserving a promotion as were Thomas Rosser, John Singleton Mosby and especially John Pelham. In June of 1862, I pushed through Rosser's colonelcy of the Fifth Virginia Cavalry. On June 23, the commission was ordered by the Secretary [of War] Rosser came to me by daylight of the next morning and I gave him the particulars. He was in my brigade and I wanted him to play an important part in the next battle. I told him to: "Come a-runnin."[42] Rosser in daily engagements with the enemy vindicated his claims as an admirable outpost commander, vigilant, active and accurate in conclusions about enemy's designs; in battle, a bold and dashing leader; on the march and in bivouac a rigid disciplinarian, but at the same time exacting the confidence of his entire command.[43] I regarded John S. Mosby as bold, daring, intelligent and discreet. The information he obtained and transmitted was relied upon and I had no doubt of his value. Since I first knew him, he never once alluded to his own rank or promotion; thus it came by the force of his own merit.[44] But, John Pelham was noble, chivalric and gallant, above all the others.

Interviewer: Why were you so adamant about John Pelham's promotion to colonel?

GEN. STUART: By mid-February 1863, I had already made several urgent recommendations for the promotion of Major John Pelham, my chief of artillery, which had not been favorably considered by the War Department. The Battle of Fredericksburg, formed a fresh chapter in his career of exploits without a parallell, I felt it to be a duty, as well as a pleasure, to earnestly repeat what I had said in his behalf, and to add that, if meritorious conduct in battle ever earned promotion, Major John Pelham of Alabama should be appointed colonel of artillery. Not only

COLONEL JOHN SINGLETON MOSBY
Massachusetts Commandery Military
Order of the Loyal Legion and the
United States Army Military History Institute

LIEUTENANT COLONEL JOHN PELHAM
Massachusetts Commandery Military
Order of the Loyal Legion and the
United States Army Military History Institute

this, but his functions as chief of artillery of the cavalry division, always, in battle, placed him where they became those of a colonel, because of the fact that much artillery was always accumulated on the flank, to enfilade and take the enemy in flank, as was done with so much execution at Groveton, Sharpsburg and Fredericksburg. Pelham's well-known ability as an artillery officer had won him the confidence of generals in command who unhesitatingly entrusted to him the artillery thus brought together from various batteries. It had been alleged that he was too young. Though remarkably youthful in appearance there were generals as young with less claim for that distinction, and no veteran in age had ever shown more coolness and better judgement in the sphere of his duty.[45]

Interviewer: It was regretable that Pelham received his colonelcy posthumously.

GEN. STUART: Yes. You must know how his death distressed me.[46] How much he was beloved, appreciated and admired . . . the tears of agony we had shed, and the gloom of mourning throughout my command beared witness.[47]

Interviewer: Did John Pelham exemplify the very embodiment of the Confederate knight, General?

GEN. STUART: He fell mortally wounded in the Battle of Kellysville, March 17, with the battle cry on his lips and the light of victory beaming from his eye. Though young in years, a mere stripling in appearance, remarkable for his genuine modesty of deportment, he yet disclosed on the battlefield the conduct of a veteran, and displayed in his handsome person the most imperturbable coolness in danger. His eye had glanced over every battlefield of this army from the first Manassas to the moment of his death, and he was, with a single exception, a brilliant actor in all. The memory of "the gallant Pelham," his many manly virtues, his noble nature and purity of character, are enshrined as a sacred legacy in hearts of all who knew him. His record was bright and spotless; his career was brilliant and successful. He fell the noblest of sacrifices on the altar of his country, to whose glorious service he had dedicated his life from the beginning of the war.[48]

Interviewer: You often signed your personal correspondence "K.G.S." What does this mean?

GEN. STUART: It was a moniker I used after I received a pair of elegant gold spurs from an anonymous lady in Baltimore. The initials stood for "Knight of the Golden Spurs."[49]

Interviewer: Did you see yourself as a knight?

GEN. STUART: Our Southern ideals of patriotism provided us with the concepts of chivalry. I tried to excell in these virtues, but others provided a truer interpretation of gallant conduct.

Interviewer: General Stuart, how would you define the phrase: "a truer interpretation of gallant conduct?"

GEN. STUART: A devoted champion of the South was one who possessed a heart intrepid, a spirit invincible, a patriotism too lofty to admit a selfish thought and a conscience that scorned to do a mean act. His legacy would be to leave a shining example of heroism and patriotism to those who survive.[50]

Interviewer: Did you ever grow weary of the war?

GEN. STUART: Yes, the responsibility of duty kept me from my family. In the fall of 1863, I wrote to my wife: Your picture is a great comfort to me as lip salve. I carry it next to my heart, but do not need it my love, to keep you ever vividly before me. As I think of you now in writing, I find my arm ready to stray from this sheet to clasp the ideal Flora. Would that it were the real, and I could give you such an old-fashioned squeeze as would make you exclaim "don't!" When shall I have that happiness? Ah when! Not till you can pay me one of those charming visits and bring the dear little pledge along to astound the staff and take Papa by storm.[51] It was always my desire that my family have a home, I wrote to my wife on another occassion: "I wish

you could get a little home of your own somewhere to have birds and flowers and books, the
very best society in the world," and when "war's
dread commotion is over," I would step quietly
into such a home and . . . but I wish an assurance
on your part in the other event of your surviving
me, that you will make the land for which I gave
my life your home, and keep my offspring on
Southern soil.[52] I was very anxious to see her
settled in a permanent home where a garden, a
yard and a household would interest and occupy
her.[53]

Interviewer: It must have been very difficult for you to maintain a close relationship with your wife and children during the course of the war. How did you
reassure your wife of your love and convince her
of your duty to the Confederate States of America?

GEN. STUART: In November of 1862, McClellan was advancing
and there was no rest for me. Dr. Brewer's dispatch came and I answered it at once. The second came, saying my darling Pet's case [daugh-
ter, Flora] was doubtful and urged me in my wife's
name to come. I received it on the field of battle.
I was at no loss to decide that it was my duty to
my wife and daughter to remain. I was entrusted
with the conduct of affairs; the issue of which
would affect my wife and children and the mothers and children of our country much more seri-
ously than we could believe.[54] I had been in battle
every day since I heard of Flora's sickness and
that was November 2. She died November 3 and
I heard of it November 6. I had been harassing
and checking a heavy force believed to be
McClellan's.[55] I was compelled by my sacred honor
to remain at my post at all cost. I tried at every
opportunity to console her. [Flora Cooke Stuart]
I wrote to her: "I would like to be gathering vio-
lets with you on the hills of the Dan [River,] but
this war is not over and you must nerve your heart
for its trials, its griefs and its woes, and let me
ask you now my dear one, partner of my joys and
sorrows, not to take me from that confidence

which I feel I deserve, that love of which I have been so proud." I entreated her to "Look not mournfully upon the past, it comes not back again, but wisely improve the present and go forth to meet the future with a bold and manly heart."[56] If we were victorious my place would be in the pursuit . . . if I fell I would leave in the sacrifice a legacy more to be prized by my children and wife than ten years of longer life with the chances and temptations that may environ me. I had no idea of sacrificing myself rashly but I hoped to do my duty with a firm reliance on divine aid to uphold me.

Interviewer: In December of 1862, the Battle of Fredericksburg ensued. What was your reaction to this campaign?

GEN. STUART: We were victorious. Repulsing the enemy's attack in main force with tremendous slaughter. General John R. Cooke was wounded in the forehead. He was in no danger and received all the attention that mother or sister could give if here. I got shot through my fur collar but was unhurt.[57] The victory won by us here was one of the neatest and cheapest of the war. With us were a few Englishmen who had surveyed Solferino and all of the battlefields of Italy. They said that the pile of dead on the plains of Fredericksburg exceeded anything of the sort ever seen by them. Fredericksburg was in ruins. It was the saddest sight I ever saw.[58]

Interviewer: In June 1863, the Richmond newspapers stated that you were surprised by Major General Alfred Pleasonton's cavalry, Brigadier General John Buford's division specifically, in this rustic vicinity of Brandy Station, where we are now located. As it turned out this engagement was the largest cavalry battle on the North American continent. Would you please comment on this statement.

GEN. STUART: Yes, I would like to comment on that statement. God had spared me through another bloody battle, and blessed with victory our arms. The fight occurred on June 9 beyond Brandy Station and

MAJOR GENERAL WILLIAM HENRY FITZHUGH LEE
*Massachusetts Commandery Military
Order of the Loyal Legion and the
United States Army Military History Institute*

was to be called the "Battle of Fleetwood Heights." We mourned the loss of Farley, my volunteer aide, killed, and White wounded painfully. Goldsborough was captured taking an important order to Wickham. General William H. F. Lee, [son of Robert E. Lee] with his whole brigade, distinguished themselves, fighting almost entirely against regulars. The papers are in great error, as usual, about the transaction. It was no surprise. The enemy's movement was known and he was defeated. We captured three pieces of artillery which the horse artillery retained. The entire loss did not exceed 500 killed, wounded and missing. Among the wounded were General William H. F. Lee, Lieutenant Colonel Phillips and Colonel Butler [whose foot was amputated]. Colonel [Peirce M. B.] Young made a splendid charge. Fitz Lee's brigade did not see much execution as it was but little engaged. The *Richmond Examiner* of June 12 lied from beginning to end. I lost no paper—no nothing—except the casualties of battle. You know, I understand the spirit and object of the detraction and can, I believe, trace the source. At any rate, by June 12, Weaver had returned from amongst the Yankees; they acknowledged themselves whipped badly.[59]

Interviewer: Since it has been such a long time now, are you sure you would not like to put closure on this "Brandy Station Controversy" once and for all?

GEN. STUART: I lost nothing whatever. The *Examiner* to the contrary notwithstanding. I believe it all originates in the Salt question.

Interviewer: What do you mean "the Salt Question"?

GEN. STUART: You must be careful now what you say. I will, of course, take no notice of such base falsehood.

Interviewer: Did the cavalry have any other confrontations prior to the Battle of Gettysburg?

GEN. STUART: Yes, in the vicinity of Aldie the entire cavalry and a large force of infantry made a forced reconnaissance on June 21. My loss in killed and wounded was several hundred, though not many killed. The

LIEUTENANT GENERAL WADE HAMPTON
Massachusetts Commandery Military
Order of the Loyal Legion and the
United States Army Military History Institute

enemy suffered very heavily. The First Dragoons tried very hard to kill me. Four officers fired deliberately at me with their pistols several times. God had spared my life and blessed us with success.[60]

Interviewer: Many people question your activities prior to the Battle of Gettysburg. Some say that you prevented a Confederate victory at that battle. How do you answer these critics?

GEN. STUART: I crossed near Dranesville and went close to Georgetown and Washington, cutting four important railroads, joining our army in time for the Battle of Gettysburg, with 900 prisoners and 200 wagons and splendid teams. I shelled Carlisle and burnt the barracks. I had been blessed with great success on this campaign and the accidents and losses in the way of captives were in no way chargeable to my command. I felt that we must invade again—it is the only path of peace. We were received well in Pennsylvania and our troops treated the population better than our own. General Lee's maueuvering the Yankees out of Virginia was the grandest piece of strategy ever heard of. My cavalry had nobly sustained its reputation and done better and harder fighting that it ever had since the war. We got the better of the fight at Gettysburg but retired because the position we took could not be held. When we gained a fresh supply of ammuntion we would give battle again.[61] If they had only sent 10,000 reinforcements and plenty of ammunition to join him [R.E. Lee] there, our recrossing would have been with banners of peace. General Hampton was severly wounded at Gettysburg, but did recover. All was harmonious with us. We had paid Stoneman in compound interest and my cavalry was the finest body of men "on the planet."[62] I had a grand time in Pennsylvania and we returned without defeat to recuperate and reinforce, when, I had no doubt that the role would be re-enacted.[63]

Interviewer: General, one last question concerning your wartime activities. What were the events leading up to your death at Yellow Tavern?

GEN. STUART: On May 11 about 2 a.m., I had just received information that the enemy was encamped at Ground Squirrel Bridge. The men said they had orders to move at 12 o'clock that night. I began moving to Ashland. I thought, if I reach that point before the enemy, I would move down the Telegraph Road. A portion of my command was following the enemy closely, and was camping at Mrs. Crenshaw's farm at the crossing of the South Anna [River]. By 6:30 a.m. the enemy had reached this point just before us, but was promptly whipped out, after a sharp fight, by Fitz Lee's [General Fitzhugh Lee, nephew of Robert E. Lee] advance, killing and capturing quite a number. General Gordon was in the rear of the enemy. I intersected the road the enemy was marching on at Yellow Tavern, at the head of the turnpike, six miles from Richmond. My men and horses were tired, hungry and jaded, but all right. The head of my column reached Yellow Tavern at 8:00 a.m. No enemy had passed. Citizens and furloughed soldiers reported them in a heavy column moving toward Dover Mills. I thought I would sweep across after them. I heard some firing toward their place of encampment about 7:00 a.m. Probably Gordon engaged them. The central road was safe to Hanover Junction. By 9:00 a.m., I had not learned whether the enemy had passed Yellow Tavern or passed near the James River. By 3:00 p.m., I reported that the enemy had Yellow Tavern and the Old Mountain Road for some distance above and had formed his column between Fredericksburg Railroad and that road. General Gordon was one and a half miles south of Chile's Tavern, on that road, and informed me that all the enemy's cavalry were massed there, none having gone toward the James River. I suggested that if we could make a combined attack on them with Hunton's brigade, I could not see how they could escape. I had attacked at once and felt confident of success. They had driven our extreme back a little, but we had been driving their rear and left [flanks].[64] I kept my artillery bearing on the dust near Yellow Tavern. I thought that the enemy may yet turn toward the James River.[65]

Interviewer: Shortly after this point you were mortally wounded. What was your last command to your men?

GEN. STUART: Go back! Go back, and do your duty as I have done mine, and our country will be safe! Go back! Go back! I had rather die than be whipped![66]

Interviewer: You had many close relationships with various relatives in your family, especially during the war. Which person tried your patience, and which could you consistently depend upon for support?

GEN. STUART: John Esten Cooke, my wife's cousin, was a mischievous scamp who would create humbug and tease my wife. He would tell her these tales of me shaving off my beard and a hand kissing affair. I convinced her of the folly of both incidents. I told her my beard flourishes like the gourd of Jonah and a poem:

> And long may it wave—
> For I ne'er will shave—
> While my Flora approves
> Still to grow it behooves—
> And "nary a hair"
> From it will I spare.
> [J.E.B. Stuart, December 1, 1861]

If she could have seen what passed in the hand kissing affair she would not, I know, have taken the slightest objection to it, and it was only by John Esten's distortions that it could have been made exceptionable. I told her: "My darling if you could know—(and I think you ought) how true I am to you and how centered in you is my every hope—and dream of earthly bliss, you would never listen to the idle twaddle of those who knowing how we love each other amuse themselves telling such outlandish yarns as the beard story to see how you would stand it.[67] When I reflect upon the anxiety that mischievous cousin has caused you for nothing, I am quite out of patience."[68] John

CAPTAIN JOHN ESTEN COOKE
(Civilian Suit)

Library of Virginia

Esten was a case and I couldn't like him.[69] But then there was Cousin Nannie, the little entrantress [Anne Overton Price]. I could confide in her; talk to her as if communing with myself. I spoke to her about my grief for little Flora.[70]

Interviewer: Can you express how you felt about your child's death?

GEN. STUART: It was nearly a year after little Flora died when my grief became overwhelming and I confided in Nannie. Ah! little did I think I was to be spared and she taken! I can think over her sweet little face, sweet temper and nature and extraordinary susceptibilites and weep like a child to think that their embodiment who loved her Pa like idolatry was now lifeless clay.[71] When farewells were said and tears had been shed—how I remember Little Flora running out after me, climbing up by my stirrup, her dear little arms clinging around my neck, with tearful kisses till forced away. I can never forget that picture, that parting, that embrace! Can you wonder at the tears that fill my eyes . . . The thought flashing through my mind at that moment, "we may not meet again." It is now vividly remembered and the gloomy apprehension rises and kindles tears in my eyes. I was just starting on the campaign against [General John] Pope and I knew that my life hung by a thread ready to be severed by any one of a thousands of death's missiles which sweep the battle plain. All this flashed through my mind; for there are moments which are like a century. I thought of the widow (there she stood before me) and the fatherless little sylph in my arms, and breathed a prayer that He who tempers the wind to the shorn lamb, would deal tenderly with mine. Ah! little did I think I was to be spared and she be taken! I felt it was all gain to her but my grief admonished me that earth had lost its chief attraction, and while it did not make me reckless, I went forth at the summons of duty and of danger with that cheerful resignation which the cold world called rashness.[72] May you never feel such a blow.[73]

Interviewer: What kept you going through the difficulty of war and the absence of family and friends?

GEN. STUART: I went forth on the uncertain future; my sabre did not leave my hands for months. I was substained in the hour of peril, with the consciousness of right, and upheld by the same Almighty Hand which thus far had covered my head in the day of battle, in whom I put my trust.[74] God had shielded me thus far from bodily harm, but I felt perfect resignation to go at His bidding and join my little Flora.[75]

Interviewer: General Stuart, we have discussed many events and people in your life. Do you have anything you would like to add before we conclude our interview?

GEN. STUART: In the begining of this interview, you asked me if I had fulfilled my destiny—I believe I will answer that question now. I lived my life with devotion to my country through a constant sense of duty and honor. I yielded to no man in the Confederacy in quantity and quality of service.[76] [or]

DEDICATION

Within this consecrated shrine,
Let gems of pure affection shine,
The old, the young, the sad, the gay,
Their offrings, and their homage pay.

While Mars with his stentorian voice,
Chimes in his dire discordant noise,
Sweet woman in angelic guise,
Give hope, and bids us fear despise.

The maid of Saragossa still,
Breathes in our cause her dauntless will,
Beyond Potomac's rock-bound shore,
Her touch bade southern cannon roar.

Joan of Arc with fierce intent,
Has oft o'er southern saddle bent,
To guide the hero o'er the plain,
And helped to Victory with her rein.

But softer than the chimes of even,
Gentler than the dews of heaven.
See her, o'er the wounded bending,
All her soothing power lending.

Soon may peace with rainbow splendor,
Crown the heroine-defender,
Through life her deeds shine forth in story,
In death receive the crown of glory.
[J.E.B. Stuart, January 28, 1864][77]

Interviewer: Thank you, General Stuart!

GEN. STUART: The pleasure was mine, thank you!

MAJOR GENERAL JAMES EWELL BROWN STUART

Endnotes

SESSION I

1. Heros Von Borcke, *Memoirs of the Confederate War for Independence,* Vol. 2 (Dayton: Morningside Press, 1985), 312.
2. Ibid., 313.
3. Adele H. Mitchell and Richard W. Bailey, interview by author, tape recording, Carlisle, Pennsylvania, 24 October 1992.
4. Ibid.
5. Ibid.
6. Adele H. Mitchell, ed., *The Letters of Major General James E. B. Stuart* (n.p., 1990), 179–183.
7. J. E. B. Stuart to George Hairston, Letter, 13 April 1852, Virginia Historical Society, Richmond, Va.
8. J. E. B. Stuart to George Hairston, Letter, 6 March 1851, Virginia Historical Society, Richmond, Va.
9. J. E. B. Stuart to George Hairston, Letter, 25 December 1851, Virginia Historical Society, Richmond, Va.
10. J. E. B. Stuart to George Hairston, Letter, 13 April 1852, Virginia Historical Society, Richmond, Va.
11. J. E. B. Stuart to Archibald Stuart, Letter, 23 December 1853, Occidental College, Los Angeles, Calif.
12. Mitchell, 179–183.

SESSION II

1. Mitchell, 179–183.
2. Ibid.
3. Ibid.
4. Ibid.
5. Mitchell, 182.
6. J. E. B. Stuart to H. K. Craig, Letter, 14 October 1859, National Archives, Washington, D.C.
7. J. E. B. Stuart to Elizabeth Letcher Pannill Stuart, Letter, 31 January 1860, Virginia Historical Society, Richmond, Va.
8. Ibid.
9. Ibid.
10. J. E. B. Stuart to Alexander Stuart Brown, Letter, 28 October 1855, Virginia Historical Society, Richmond, Va.
11. Flora Cooke Stuart to Beverley B. Munford, Letter, 28 March 1908, Virginia Historical Society, Richmond, Va.

12. Ibid.

13. J. E. B. Stuart to J. A. Thompson, Letter, 12 July 1860, National Archives, Washington, D.C.

14. Ibid.

15. Mitchell, 183.

16. J. E. B. Stuart to Henry Hill, Letter, 11 January 1861, University of Virginia, Charlottesville, Va.

17. Ibid.

18. J. E. B. Stuart to Lorenzo Thomas, Letter, 3 May 1861, National Archives, Washington, D.C.

SESSION III

1. J. E. B. Stuart to Flora Cooke Stuart, Letter, 12 June 1863, Virginia Historical Society, Richmond, Va.

2. J. E. B. Stuart to Flora Cooke Stuart, Letter, 9 May 1861, Emory University, Atlanta, Ga.

3. John Esten Cooke, *War Notes-January 26-May 12, 1863*, Duke University, Durham, N.C.

4. J. E. B. Stuart to Flora Cooke Stuart, Letter, 9 May 1861, Emory University, Atlanta, Ga.

5. Mitchell, 200-201.

6. Ibid., 200.

7. Ibid., 205-206.

8. J. E. B. Stuart to Flora Cooke Stuart, Letter, 19 May 1861, Museum of the Confederacy, Richmond, Va.

9. J. E. B. Stuart to John R. Cooke, Letter, 18 January 1862, Southern Historical Collection, University of North Carolina, Chapel Hill, N.C.

10. J. E. B. Stuart to Flora Cooke Stuart, Letter, 1 December 1861, Emory University, Atlanta, Ga.

11. Mitchell, 252.

12. J. E. B. Stuart to Flora Cooke Stuart, Letter, 8 April 1863, Virginia Historical Society, Richmond, Va.

13. James Mc Pherson, *Battle Cry of Freedom* (New York: Oxford Press, 1988), 297.

14. Mitchell, 206-207.

15. Ibid., 265.

16. Ibid., 208.

17. J. E. B. Stuart to Flora Cooke Stuart, Letter, 4 July 1861, Emory University, Atlanta, Ga.

18. Mitchell, 210.

19. Ibid., 210-213.

20. Ibid., 214-215.

21. Ibid., 215-218.

22. John W. Thomason, Jr., *Jeb Stuart* (New York: Charles Scribner's Sons, 1930), 120.

23. Mitchell, 218.

24. J. E. B. Stuart to Flora Cooke Stuart, Letter, 20 November 1861, Emory University, Atlanta, Ga.

25. Ibid., 238.

26. J. E. B. Stuart to Laura Ratcliffe, Letter, 25 December 1861, Library of Congress, Washington, D.C.

27. J. E. B. Stuart to Flora Cooke Stuart, Letter, 8 February 1864, Virginia Historical Society, Richmond, Va.

28. Ibid.

29. Mitchell, 252.

30. J. E. B. Stuart to Flora Cooke Stuart, Letter, Letter, 9 May 1862, Museum of the Confederacy, Richmond, Va.

31. John Esten Cooke, *Journals and Memorandum, June–July, 1862*, Duke University, Durham, N.C.

32. Mitchell, 267.

33. Ibid., 268–269.

34. Ibid., 257.

35. J. E. B. Stuart to Flora Cooke Stuart, Letter, 19 August 1862, Virginia Historical Society, Richmond, Va.

36. Henry Kyd Douglas, *I Rode with Stonewall* (Chapel Hill: University of North Carolina Press, 1940),133–134.

37. J. E. B. Stuart to Flora Cooke Stuart, Letter, 21 October 1861, Emory University Atlanta, Ga.

38. J. E. B. Stuart to R. H. Chilton, Letter, 21 May 1863, Virginia Historical Society, Richmond, Va.

39. J. E. B. Stuart to Robert E. Lee, Letter, 24 October 1862, Virginia Historical Society, Richmond, Va.

40. J. E. B. Stuart to R. H. Chilton, Letter, 4 February 1863, Virginia Historical Society, Richmond, Va.

41. J. E. B. Stuart to Robert E. Lee, Letter, 10 September 1863, Virginia Historical Society, Richmond, Va.

42. J. E. B. Stuart to Thomas Rosser, Letter, 23 June 1862, University of Virginia, Charlottesville, Va.

43. J. E. B. Stuart to Samuel Cooper, Letter, 13 January 1863, Virginia Historical Society, Richmond, Va.

44. J. E. B. Stuart to Thomas J. Jackson, Letter, 19 July 1862, Museum of the Confederacy, Richmond, Va.

45. J. E. B. Stuart to Samuel Cooper, Letter, 10 February 1863, Virginia Historical Society, Richmond, Va.

46. J. E. B. Stuart to Flora Cooke Stuart, Letter, 19 March 1863, Virginia Historical Society, Richmond, Va.

47. J. E. B. Stuart to J. L. M. Curry, Letter, 18 March 1863, Virginia Historical Society, Richmond, Va.

48. Mitchell, 301.

49. J. E. B. Stuart to Lilly Parran Lee, Letter, 5 December 1862, Duke University, Durham, N.C.

50. J. E. B. Stuart to R. H. Chilton, Letter, 3 December 1862, Virginia Historical Society, Richmond, Va.

51. Mitchell, 339.

52. J. E. B. Stuart to Flora Cooke Stuart, Letter, 19 March 1863, Virginia Historical Society, Richmond, Va.

53. J. E. B. Stuart to Flora Cooke Stuart, Letter, 27 January 1864, Virginia Historical Society, Richmond, Va.

54. J. E. B. Stuart to Flora Cooke Stuart, Letter, 2 November 1862, Virginia Historical Society, Richmond, Va.

55. J. E. B. Stuart to Flora Cooke Stuart, Letter, 6 November 1862, Virginia Historical Society, Richmond, Va.

56. Mitchell, 307.

57. Ibid., 284.

58. J. E. B. Stuart to George Washington Custis Lee, 18 December 1862, Duke University, Durham, N.C.

59. J. E. B. Stuart to Flora Cooke Stuart, Letter, 12 June 1863, Virginia Historical Society, Richmond, Va.

60. J. E. B. Stuart to Flora Cooke Stuart, Letter, 23 June 23, 1863, Virginia Historical Society, Richmond, Va.

61. Mitchell, 327.

62. J. E. B. Stuart to Flora Cooke Stuart, Letter, 13 July 1863, Virginia Historical Society, Richmond, Va.

63. Mitchell, 327.

64. J. E. B. Stuart to Braxton Bragg, Letter, 11 May 1864, 2:00 AM, 6:30 AM, 11:00 AM, 3:00 PM, Virginia Historical Society, Richmond, Va.

65. Mitchell, 393.

66. Thomason, 499.

67. J. E. B. Stuart to Flora Cooke Stuart, Letter, 1 December 1861, Emory University, Atlanta, Ga.

68. J. E. B. Stuart to Flora Cooke Stuart, Letter, 4 December 1861, Emory University, Atlanta, Ga.

69. J. E. B. Stuart to Flora Cooke Stuart, Letter, 11 December 1861, Emory University, Atlanta, Ga.

70. Mitchell, 344.

71. J. E. B. Stuart to Lilly Parren Lee, Letter, 16 November 1862, Duke University, Durham, N.C.

72. Mitchell, 343–344.

73. J. E. B. Stuart to Lilly Parren Lee, Letter, 16 November 1862, Duke University, Durham, N.C.

74. J. E. B. Stuart to Flora Cooke Stuart, Letter, 8 April 1863, Virginia Historical Society, Richmond, Va.

75. J. E. B. Stuart to Flora Cooke Stuart, Letter, 6 November 1862, Virginia Historical Society, Richmond, Va.

76. J. E. B. Stuart to Alexander R. Boteler, Letter, 6 February 1864, Duke University, Durham, N.C.

77. J. E. B. Stuart to Flora Cooke Stuart, Letter, 30 January 1864, Virginia Historical Society, Richmond, Va.

Bibliography

Published Works

Douglas, Henry Kyd. *I Rode with Stonewall*. Chapel Hill: University of North Carolina Press, 1940.

McPherson, James M. *Battle Cry of Freedom*. New York: Oxford Press, 1988.

Mitchell, Adele H. (ed.) *The Letters of Major General James E. B. Stuart*, n.p., 1990.

Thomason, John W., Jr. *Jeb Stuart*. New York: Charles Scribner's Sons, 1930.

Von Borcke, Heros. *Memoirs of the Confederate War for Independence*. Dayton: Morningside, Press, 1985.

Unpublished Works

Bailey, Richard, Ph.D. *Letter to Bernice-Marie Yates,* March 2, 1993, Author's Collection.

Cooke, John Esten. *Journals and Memorandum, June–July, 1862*. Durham: Special Collections Library, Duke University.

———. *War Notes, January 26–May 12, 1863*. Durham: Special Collections Library, Duke University.

Mitchell, Adele H., and Richard W. Bailey. Interview, tape recording. Carlisle, Pennsylvania, October 24, 1992.

Stuart, Flora Cooke. *Letter to Beverley B. Munford, March 28, 1908*. Richmond: Manuscript Collection, James Ewell Brown Stuart Papers, Virginia Historical Society.

Stuart, James Ewell Brown. *Letter to Colonel Alexander R. Boteler, February 6, 1864*. Richmond: Manuscript Collection, James Ewell Brown Stuart Papers, Virginia Historical Society.

———. *Letters to General Braxton Bragg, May 11, 1864: 2:00 AM, 6:30 AM, 11:00 AM, 3:00 PM*. Richmond: Manuscript Collection, James Ewell Brown Stuart Papers, Virginia Historical Society.

———. *Letters to General R. H. Chilton, December 3, 1862, December 21, 1862, February 4, 1863.* Richmond: Manuscript Collection, James Ewell Brown Stuart Papers, Virginia Historical Society.

———. *Letter to Brigadier General John R. Cooke, January 18, 1862.* Chapel Hill: Southern Historical Collection, University of North Carolina.

———. *Letters to General Samuel Cooper, January 13, 1863 and February 10, 1863.* Richmond: Manuscript Collection, James Ewell Brown Stuart Papers, Virginia Historical Society.

———. *Letter to Colonel H. K. Craig, October 14, 1859.* Washington, D.C.: National Archives.

———. *Letter to Congressman J. L. M. Curry of Alabama, March 18, 1863.* Richmond: Manuscript Collection, James Ewell Brown Stuart Papers, Virginia Historical Society.

———. *Letters to George Hairston, March 6, 1851, December 25, 1851, April 13, 1852.* Richmond: Manuscript Collections: James Ewell Brown Stuart Papers, Virginia Historical Society.

———. *Letter to Major Henry Hill, January 11, 1861.* Charlottesville: Special Collections, University of Virginia.

———. *Letter to General Thomas J. Jackson, July 19, 1862.* Richmond: Eleanor S. Brockenbrough Library, The Museum of the Confederacy.

———. *Letter to Major General George Washington Custis Lee, December 18, 1862.* Durham: Special Collections Library, Duke University.

———. *Letter to Lilly Parren Lee, December 5, 1862.* Durham: Special Collections Library, Duke University.

———. *Letters to General Robert E. Lee, October 24, 1862 and September 10, 1863.* Richmond: Manuscript Collection, James Ewell Brown Stuart Papers, Virginia Historical Society.

———. *Letter to Laura Radcliffe, December 25, 1861.* Washington, D.C.: Library of Congress.

———. *Letter to Colonel Thomas Rosser, January 23, 1862.* Charlottesville: Special Collections, University of Virginia.

———. *Letter to Archibald Stuart, December 23, 1853.* Los Angeles: Special Collections, Occidental College.

———. *Letter to Elizabeth Letcher Pannill Stuart, January 30, 1860.* Richmond: Manuscript Collection, James Ewell Brown Stuart Papers, Virginia Historical Society.

———. *Letters to Flora Cooke Stuart, May 9, 1861, July 4, 1861, October 21, 1861, November 6, 1861, November 24, 1861, December 1, 1861, December 11, 1861, December 12, 1861.* Atlanta: Special Collections, Emory University.

———. *Letters to Flora Cooke Stuart, May 19, 1861 and May 9, 1862.* Richmond: Eleanor S. Brockenbrough Library, The Museum of the Confederacy.

———. *Letters to Flora Cooke Stuart, March 19, 1862, November 2, 1862, August 19, 1862, November 6, 1862, March 18, 1863, March 19, 1863, April 8, 1863, June 12, 1863, June 23, 1863, July 13, 1863, July 19, 1863, January 27, 1864.* Richmond: Manuscript Collection, James Ewell Brown Stuart Papers, Virginia Historical Society.

———. *Letter to Flora Cooke Stuart, October 3, 1863.* Washington, D.C.: Library of Congress.

———. *Letter to Colonel Lorenzo Thomas, May 3, 1861.* Washington, D.C.: National Archives.

———. *Letter to Lieutenant J. A. Thompson Adjutant, July 12, 1860.* Washington, D.C.: National Archives.

INDEX